Night Vision

Also by John Foy:

Techne's Clearinghouse

December 31, 2018
New York

Night Vision

POEMS

~~John~~ Foy

[signature]

WINNER OF THE NEW CRITERION POETRY PRIZE

To Robert,
A friend in
youth, and now
a friend in
fatherhood.

St. Augustine's Press
SOUTH BEND, IN

Best
[signature]

Funding for this year's New Criterion Poetry Prize
has been provided by Joy & Michael Millette

Library of Congress Cataloging-in-Publication Data
Foy, John, 1960- author.
Night vision / John Foy.
First edition.
South Bend, Indiana: St. Augustine's Press, 2016.
LCCN 2016033736
ISBN 9781587315701 (hardback)
BISAC: POETRY; General.
LCC PS3606.O959 .A6 2016
DDC 811/.6–dc23
LC record available at https://lccn.loc.gov/2016033736

Contents

for Majô, Catherine, and Chris

Acknowledgments

I would like to thank the editors of the following publications and websites, where some of these poems first appeared:

Alabama Literary Review: "Night Vision" and "Suboptimal"
American Arts Quarterly: "Killing Things"
Barrow Street: "Dog"
Cimarron Review: "Tracers" and "Grave" (both from the sequence "The Book of Common Tasks")
The Dark Horse: "Woods"
The Hopkins Review: "Going Out of Eden"
The Hudson Review: "Sorrow, Meister Eckhart Said" and "Why Is It?"
The Nebraska Review: "Sunlight on the Snow Today" and "Night Heron"
The New Criterion: "Son of Telamon" and "Terminal"
Parnassus Poetry in Review: "On Fame," "My New Guitar," and "Room"
The Raintown Review: "Hook Road, Delaware River" and "Deer Rifle"
Stealing Time: "Nothing Can Happen"
Think Journal: "Rio de Janeiro"
The Village Voice: "Grinder"
The Yale Review: "The White-Breasted Nuthatch"

Online:
Angle: "Jovian"
823 on High: "Few Days" and "Fermi's Paradox"
Kin: "My Personal Relationship with Christ"
Linebreak: "Wild Turkeys"
The Nervous Breakdown: "Condolences"
YARN: "Soccer Field, Wards Island" and "OK, Chris"

"Deer Rifle" was reprinted in *The Best of the Raintown Review* anthology.
"The White-Breasted Nuthatch" appeared on *Poetry Daily*, November 25, 2015.

Night Vision

I

Deer Rifle

for my uncle, John McWilliams

The .22-caliber crack was clear
and light, and the bullet that it sent
was gone, went out, away, and you could hear
right after that unquestioning report
the piece of charcoal burst apart,
the very thing that you were aiming for
blasted to bits at fifty yards. The art
of picking off briquettes and wooden boards
was what you taught me as a boy,
the craft of clarity and range, and how
to hit the target cleanly and destroy.
I see it in my mind so clearly now,
you helping me to stand steady, breathe,
and look upon what's out there and believe.

Killing Things

Maybe you'd agree that Robert Frost
was lucky not to task the flesh of birds
his tractor ran across. The worst they got
was just a scare that left their nest exposed.
So he and daughter tried to keep it right
and cover them with ferns, but even he
would never know if they survived that night.

It was a hedgehog Philip Larkin killed,
though by mistake. He actually went outside
to mow the lawn, like any man, and caught
this creature in the blades—the one he'd fed.
What in the end could be more Larkinesque?
He should have been more careful, but at least
the hedgehog's death was instantaneous.

When Wilbur accidentally killed a toad,
it was the power mower once again.
He clipped its leg, and off it went to die
beneath a cineraria. He used
the words "ebullient" and "emperies"
to talk about the life he'd compromised.
What would Philip Larkin think of these?

When my turn came, it happened in a field.
I hadn't known that I'd gone over it,
but there it was, a rabbit much the worse
for having been beneath the rotor blades.
I'd laid its back right open to the bone,

but it was still alive and looked at me,
and then I had to kill it with a stone.

Fire and Forget

i Apaches

We reached out to you
in attack helicopters
and killed you at speed
in low-level combat runs,
chain guns jackhammering
and missiles locked on where you were.
We went in hard
and didn't care, then, what we did,
damaged in battle
but coming back and going in,
working with Marines below
in the deep, bitter zones
to make sure everything was gone.

ii Door Gunner

My hands had gloves on
because the grip was hot,
the guns we had on board
pouring down points of light,
the lights that I let go
going down to put the earth
to dancing, the dust
settling on what didn't survive
and never had a chance.
Forgive me if you can
for what I did to you,
and know it falls to me
to think about that ruined road.

iii Deep-Strike Fighters

They go to what they have to kill
in air-to-ground attacks
a hundred miles away,
but all the thrill is gone, the game
gone on too long now,
the ghostly lights of the battle group
and the going in deep, the deep-strike
fighters going in
to take out targets living
only as coordinates
that light up briefly in the dark
on cockpit screens—but down there too
in the night, a gleam, gone.

Tracers

The tracers always look as though
they want so badly just to get
to where it is they're going,

leaping incandescently
with a will the mind has given them,
reaching across as a hand would

to touch what it most desires
and wants, now, to search and probe.
They just go out and light up

the night, all blue and brutal,
and light up what they light upon,
and the deed is quickly done.

Grave

Go out to where the wasted are,
and do what you're assigned to do.
Look for mines and booby traps

that might be under the remains,
and when it's safe to go ahead,
put the remains inside a pouch

and dig a grave that's four-feet deep
and put the pouch inside the grave.
With deliberation, under the sky,

knowing this really has no end,
shovel back in gently
the earth you dug to make the grave.

Son of Telamon

after Homer, The Odyssey, *Book XI*

Sick with fear by the blood hole,
I saw the fighters dragging round
their gory combat gear, each one
craving recognition, sympathy,
so many of them still amazed,
going through the dark.

Here came one, an old friend, slowly,
whispering now in a voice I used to know,
coming to plead that I set up his oar
atop a cairn along the beach,
in memory of a simple man and the good work
he used to do in the waves.

Then my mother came, my mother,
remote among the houseless dead, those ghosts
that hung about in silence by the blood.
I cried for her. I cried for the futility
of my embrace where all was only
the negative image of what used to be.

Then the Rock Thrower came, Son of Telamon,
standing apart, bemired and bemused.
Even here, though I called to him by name,
Aias would not speak to me and turned away
and went back deeper into Erebos.
Who would ever call him by his name again?

Few Days

How lucky that nature's not around the bend
or apoplectic and doesn't ever need
fentanyl or dope to make the end
more bearable. Things do die violently,
of course, but hurt is never the intent.
The creatures of the field, even the bugs,
they all must all eat—each other. That moment
when the quick is rendered into food—a plug
of meat, some bloody ribs, or just a bare
bone—is hard for us, but a chinchilla
in the Andes isn't poor and won't despair
at being eaten up. It isn't thrilled
at getting caught, but the moment soon passes
like the shadow of a cloud along the cliffs.

Night Vision

You'll never see it if you look
directly at it in the dark.
It's just a shifting, black
on black, something just

a part of the perimeter,
no claim upon it as it comes
along the bales of razor wire
deftly and alone,

and it is near you now, has
somehow gotten in, at peace
with what it does
in the darkness, and why.

II

Soccer Field, Wards Island

You don't care about the cold,
and you don't care about the wind
coming off Hell Gate since dawn
that has kept even the gulls away,
and you don't care that you have to play
on a field again that's hard
and unlovely and unforgiving
(but fair, too, in its gravel and glass).
This is what it is to fight
not far from a House for the Mad
under the Triborough Bridge, on a pitch
where big kids from Pelham come
to bring you down, but you beat them
in the dirt here, in the cold.

OK, Chris

OK, Chris. Go out and hit the ball
just like you did in practice yesterday.
Step into it and drive it off the wall
in center field, or swing away
and put it out there in the gap in left,
and watch out for the hanging curve. If you
can see it coming, wait for it
to break, then knock the sucker black and blue.
Get under it, and it's as good as gone.
If you can get to second, go in hard
and try to wreck the throw that's coming in.
Let the shortstop know that life is hard.
Just listen for my voice out there, and know
I'm with you. I'll tell you when to go.

Nothing Can Happen

Nothing, really, can happen to you.
Everything is going to be all right.
That hunting rifle on the wall,
the Remington, wasn't loaded
when we looked at it last night,
and the big, stainless steel
carving knife from Cooks Club
is safe behind the butcher block.
That Chinese family, the Wangs, who keep
to themselves but are nice enough,
probably won't ever think
of killing themselves outright
by burning coals in a bucket in the sink
so that carbon monoxide fumes
go into the room where the children sleep.
And that man we know in 16-B
who got roughed up at knifepoint
in the lobby of our building—he is fine.
There wasn't that much blood,
and the security cameras got on film
the five men who assaulted him.
They won't be back here for a while.

Nothing, really, can happen to you.
Everything is going to be all right.
You'll have what you need, and probably more.
That old man we always see
in the nursing home when we go
to visit Grandma in her room,

Mr. Wenzel is his name,
he doesn't always heave and roar
when the nurses put the pureed peas
and turkey paste into his mouth.
His mouth is open anyway,
and it looks as though he's gone to sleep
when he sits there in the dining room
with his head back. He doesn't mind.
The nurses here, of course, are kind.

Grandma's glad, I'm sure, to have
the dextrose and sodium chloride bags
hooked up there beside her bed.
Oh, and the dollop of scrambled egg
she gets in the morning is hot enough,
and the Boost she drinks five times a day
will bloat her only for a while.
The cost, so far, is manageable.
The nurses, as I said, are kind.
They clean out Grandma's catheter
as often as they can, and now
insurance covers most of it.

Nothing at all can happen to you.
Everything is going to be all right.
The war goes on, but keep in mind
that not all soldiers get burned up
or blown apart and filled with holes.
They kill insurgents over there,
and all the ones who get shot up
are people who'd die anyway.

I don't think you will have to fight.
The war will be over soon,
and no one, then, is going to care
about who did what to whom, or why.
So forget about these things, the guns.
We've put your money in mutual funds.

Elementary School

Now, everyone hold hands and close your eyes.
I need the first in line to take my hand,
and then we all go out. It's time to go.
We're going through this room, then down the hall
through broken glass, but please keep your eyes closed
and do not push. We're going by the gym.
Then we'll walk up to the firehouse.
We're going to wait there, in the firehouse,
until your parents come to pick you up.
They'll get here quickly, that I promise you.
The ambulances here have come to help.
And look. Police are here to help, with dogs.
Before you know it, you'll be home. About
the others, well, we have to wait and see.

Going Out of Eden

My son was troubled by Masaccio,
the one of Eve and Adam ushered out
of Eden, crying, side by side, a sorrow
clear to all and leaving little doubt
that what had happened to them wasn't good.
It was for him a point of fascination
that God could get so mad. He understood
that they were naked, cold, and couldn't run.

But where was Eden? Where, then, would they go,
and why couldn't they get some clothes to wear?
"It's like a place in the mind," I said, "although
some people think it used to be right here
in this world." Then he went away to go
and play with the dogs in the rain and didn't care.

Hook Road, Delaware River

By 10:00 a.m. the sun is high enough
to shine down into the water where
the bottom on the far side drops off

into shelving limestone slabs, the "stairs,"
where large-mouth bass and walleyes keep
their counsel in the dark. No one dares

to swim those deeper reaches
but a few local boys, who know
what the river's like in that stretch

on the Pennsylvania side below
the cliffs that go from this world
into still waters where the current slows

above the deepest trench. It's true
each summer some kid drowns, but still you love
the sky, the depths, the water's moods

that take and carry you and prove
your understanding of what you've chosen
to be in, be it pools or a groove

between rocks where water shoots, loaded
with the force of what's inevitably
still to come. My two children go

in the hot sun along a stony
path upstream to the railroad bridge,
to play at keeping all the crazy

river junk they've found. There on a ledge
categorized and displayed
along the stone trestle's edge

where the water is shallow enough to wade:
sinkers, bobbers, hooks, and bright lures
lost like souls but good enough to save.

A child feels, under blue
skies here, like a rock-and-river god
diving for golf balls, happy to do

whatever the river asks. It's understood
that being in the river is to be
a part of it. This summer it's been good

to go out where the shelf drops into deep
water and dive in and swim free
of whatever it was I was supposed to be.

Sorrow, Meister Eckhart Said

Sorrow, Meister Eckhart said,
comes of wanting what you cannot have,
and of wanting there is no end.
But what then does it mean

to say I want the world for you?
Not everything's available,
and of what is, there's much
you really would not want.

The burning jet fuel coming down
like rain does no one any good,
and the clear linear beauty
of rocket fire pouring down

upon some godforsaken hill
is death to some. And the grief
of *loving* what you cannot have,
a girl maybe, a way of life,

takes its sorry place in line
behind the horrors that arrive
inevitably like older boys
who've spent time in prison.

What I want doesn't seem
ever to have had a lot
to do with anything, but here
is what I want for you:

an educated, peaceful life
among the modest and the sane
but close enough to true toil
to know what it takes and takes away.

I'd like to fill your mind
with Eliot and teach you to love
the feel of infield dirt,
and I don't want you to die,

but coffee in the cold dawn
is good, and you may be called upon
to fight, and sorrow has a way
of coming out to find you.

Sunlight on the Snow Today

Sunlight on the snow today
brings the brightness of a sword,
and the wind here, in the field,
says only tactical things

in among what sticks are left
pointing up through the snow.
The old birdhouse has had enough,
its eye poked out, reason gone,

the post it's long been nailed to
leaning over now, in the wind,
like one who'd surely go away
if such a thing were possible.

The juncos never go away.
Beyond the point of caring,
they carry out the bitter tasks
their bitter days require.

From even farther out, I hear
the imprecations of the best
Arctic fighters, my children
on maneuvers in the far field.

III

Englewood

I'm still here,
we are all still here
where you used to be.
I'm sorry to have to say
we've had to make arrangements
to sell the house in Englewood.
Penny, Jennifer, and I,
we are doing what we have to do
to clean it out, get it ready
to go later this year.
It is not possible, I hope
you understand, to keep
everything that's in there now.
We've had to bring a dumpster in.
It is not easy, but the time
we spend there in the house
is like time still spent with you.
I'm learning now, at last,
what you knew all along,
that to *be* means only to be used up
by those who need you most.
If it is somehow granted
in the cool porticos of Heaven
still to feel what happens here below,
then know we think of you,
it's April, baseball has begun,
and I am here, standing in
the kitchen where you stood.
The white-throated sparrow

gives up its seven-note song, and it rained
last night. It rained hard down here
where you used to be.

The Answering Machine

Hello, John. This is Father McRay.
I'm from the hospice, and I'm
the bereavement specialist.
I'm calling to see how you are coping
with your mother's death, how you're getting along.
If you need additional resources on
the nature and process of grieving,
you can call the 1-800 number, night or day.
May the Lord be with you and guide you
on your bereavement journey.

Oh, Father McRay, fuck you and stick
your bereavement journey up your ass.
We all have to die, and what
you've found to say is not enough.

Condolences

How can I help you with your grief,
though maybe I shouldn't even try
if truth be told. There's no relief
really. Your mother had to die
someday, and how unfit
a man you'd be if you couldn't make
believe you were tough enough to take it
and move on, how fake
the higher calculus, being
at peace and all that. You've lost
her now, few care, and nothing
can help, and no one knows the cost
you've paid—but everyone knows
we die like dogs in the deep snow.

Why Is It?

Why is it I keep these things,
this calendar, a pocket kind,
the pages filled with random jottings
that might have mattered at the time
scribbled in and barely legible,
but clear enough to understand
on the fly back then, now valuable
only to show again the plans
that used to have significance,
or the name of a girl in Carson City
who never called me back, or a list
from five years ago today,
a week before my mother died,
of some vegetables I had to buy?

Hudson

I went out walking just to be
by the river for a while, to be
alone by the water, in the wind
kicking up whitecaps
in the cold, because I wanted
to be out along a footpath
in the cold watching a black
tug go by, its bridge
all wind-eaten white, and a black
barge with cargo stacked up
in red containers on the deck,
the winter work just going on,
and Jersey, over there,
lost in a petrochemical dream.

Suboptimal

I dwell at night among devices
that are linked up now in the dark
and sometimes come alive
with lights, blinking on my desk
to indicate another message coming in
from a suboptimal world
I don't much feel like living in
tonight, wanting only, like a child,
to pull the covers up and close my eyes
to cables and wires and the online
lie and the rigged life they try
to make me think is uncompromised and mine
and beyond anyone's asking how this
makes better what's left of my hours.

My Personal Relationship with Christ

So let me say up front I've never had
a personal relationship with Christ,
although Lord knows I've tried. For instance, when
my mother died, I went to write her name
in the Book of the Dead at Corpus Christi Church.
I carefully inscribed it on the page
and in that devastating darkness wished
that He had come to talk with me. I prayed
for quick conveyance of my mother's soul,
but what Christ may have done to comfort her,
wherever she might have been, I never knew.
I've often wondered what it would be like
to have a drink with Him. Would He show up
at Mulligan's or at the Old Town bar?
He wouldn't take a whiskey, only wine.
I'd treat Him to a round or two. The point
is that He never comes, which makes it hard
to have a personal relationship.
Maybe I should go to Abilene
and get a gun, a Bushmaster assault rifle,
and learn to sing some Randy Travis tunes
and send my money in to men of God
like Creflo Dollar and his ministry.
In righteousness and rhinestones maybe then
Christ would come to me. It would be good
to have this personal relationship,
but how does anybody pal around
with the nexus of all human suffering?
And why would He decide to hang around

and listen to my low-end grievances?
To think He would is to be guilty of
the sin of pride, or at the very least
to be unpleasantly presumptuous.
If everyone is special, no one is,
and I would bet that Jesus doesn't want
a personal relationship with me.

Terminal

What if, past a certain point, it weren't
so bad to die? What if it were like
lying on a couch at 3:00 a.m.,
the mind aloft and quiet, given over
to a few piano notes finding ways
melodically through predetermined loops
in Brian Eno's *Music for Airports*?
That's what you'd be listening to,
music for those places where we go
to go away, the music of going away,
and you just disappearing into it
without effort or pain,
finding peace in knowing *to obey*
means at its root only to listen.

IV

Jovian

Jupiter, its moons, and a space probe

i

The ones you loved are all in orbit now,
although they're not exactly what they were
when you took pleasure with them here on Earth.
You are, at last, a great monstrosity,
and they your Galilean satellites
that bear the names of those you lusted for
when everything was young. Your gravity
ensures that what comes close to you will die.

So what we look to mostly are the moons.
Europa keeps her distance, caked in ice,
her prebiotic waters deeper down.
She has endured your looming over her
for more than ninety-seven million years,
and still, we don't know how, her face is clear.

ii

Poor Io, who'd have thought you'd come to this?
You got a thoroughgoing feel for it
in olden days when Jupiter came down
to rectify his otherworldly will.
You bore the brunt, a fetching, pure-white cow,
till Juno came to vet the goings-on
and saw right through the bovine stratagem.
She put the fly on you to drive you mad.

And now? Volcanoes pock your pizza-face,
four hundred of them, each a sulfurous wound
releasing vile ejecta into space.
The only things that penetrate you now
are lines of Jupiter's magnetic field.
Your life perhaps was better as a cow.

iii

Europa, the aristocrat. You wore
a coriander tunic on the beach
that afternoon, and when a bull came round,
you touched his horn, and then . . . well, then you got
ahold of it like any randy girl,
and off you went. You took the bull in stride
without a thought for bestiality
and ended up in Crete, a riven queen.

And now, though just a moon, you're thought to be
the smoothest object in the universe,
the only hope we have of other life.
You cannot disengage from Jupiter,
but he won't ever feel the warmth again
or go inside the hydrothermal vents.

iv

We won't forget you, Ganymede, a boy
too close to too much power far too soon,
but what advantage now, and where's the cup?
You traded in your krater for the craters
that run across your sad, bombarded face.
It's dear, the cost of favor with the gods.
You wonder if your dogs still bark for you
at night around the farm. I doubt they do.

Your gaze is fixed now on the Great Red Spot,
which brings to mind a ravaged orifice
unconscionably tried from age to age,
a site of much anxiety, but then
the gods don't really care. You were a boy
and unprepared for these enormities.

V

The name Callisto meant "most beautiful,"
and Aeschylus once wrote a tragedy
about your plight. The work was later lost.
You wanted to live life in such a way
that in your book of changes, nothing would,
but through no fault of yours, your comeliness
inflamed the huge mind of Jupiter,
who forced himself upon you in the woods.

Forget about that girl you used to be.
An awful planetary load presides
forever in the sky. You turn to him
a face that's cratered and extremely old,
a frigid lithosphere that has repelled
whatever love for you there might have been.

vi

the space probe

What is it, Juno? Why have you come back
to visit Jupiter? So much went wrong,
and after so much time what's left to say?
Your husband is a dead gas giant now,
encircled by some sixty-seven moons
that can't appeal to him or slip away.
There's nothing untoward here anymore.
You, too, perhaps have made a compromise.

You are a spacecraft now, an artifact
embarked upon a one-way trip to look
your antipathetic other in the eye.
You'll go around him more than thirty times
and then drop down, unbearable though it be,
to feel again the might of his command.

Grinder

Not good, your playing hockey with my heart.
How fast you worked it on around in front
and fed it forward to the point, this part
of me you slapped away, without a thought
that what went skittering across the ice
was not a puck, although it looked like one,
so black and vulcanized. But no. A piece
of me it was you dumped into the zone.
You laid it back along the wall out wide,
controlling it the way you wanted to,
then skated in and checked me from behind
and took a ricochet and tipped it through,
a garbage goal. That's all you ever scored,
and me, a grinder bleeding by the boards.

On Fame

loosely after a poem of the same name by John Keats

There she goes, a good-time girl
turning her tan and lovely back
on those who have not learned
to get along without her.
Now she's driving off at speed
beside some lesser man
in a BMW up Beverly Drive,
disavowing the dusty miles
and our nights in the canyon,
how she'd grip the bed and laugh.
But still I look, and still
the summer evening lights
from here to Santa Clarita
(so much pretty destitution)
try to tell me why I came
and how it still might be
and how the cost of having her
is reckoned in so many hands.
I'm going back to Laramie.
I've got a job there, a place to stay.

Rio de Janeiro

What can I find to say to you
that you haven't heard before, in rooms
by the beach in Botafogo at night
under this or that moon?

Others have found things to say,
but what does it matter
to you whose lines are like
cascading water?

What are you looking for
in the sunlight here that spills
like your own light
on this road high in the hills?

What is it I could say
that you would let me
lie down with you
deep among the trees?

Come Live with Me

after Christopher Marlowe

Come live with me, and be my love,
and get a job that pays enough
so that, together, we might buy
a house out near Redondo Beach.

Or let us sit here on a dock
and watch the tug boats going by
and not be worried overmuch
that time and money disappear.

No blue Ferrari. Not for me.
Instead, I will apply myself
to all the wan and tedious things
the world declares are practical.

And you, though not a lawyer, have
the intellect to recognize
that heron by the water's edge
as one we can depend upon.

Let's take account of what we have
in this uncluttered idiom
and tell whatever lies we may,
and then it's time for Taco Bell.

Perhaps we'll never own a home
in Malibu, or anywhere,

and summer's nearly gone, but still
come live with me, and be my love.

Rue Saint-Dominique

Rue Saint-Dominique I think it was.
You wore a dress but had no panties on
and sat beside me, sweating, in the cab.
How tactfully you hitched your dress a bit
so I could slide my left hand under you.
Well, that was what you wanted me to do.
You were intent on being touched,
as I was equally intent,
and under there you opened up
just like a sea anemone.
We'd met in a café that afternoon.
You liked Kandinsky, and we drank Médoc.
I cannot quite recall your name,
but what we wanted was the same.

A Deer

The tale is told. A hunt, a deer, the wind,
and things given to happening in the woods.
The druids thought that if you met a hind
deep within the forest, it was good
and meant you'd come in contact with a soul.
For Wyatt, deer were women of the world
who came to him at night, and one of those,
the loveliest, ran off into the wild,
leaving him, as deer did all the time,
perplexed and sad.
                    There's nothing to be done.
I look at cloven footprints left behind
along this path I go down on my own,
but I was *in* the woods. I saw the deer.
She came to me and let me handle her.

My New Guitar

My new guitar leans against the wall
like a woman who's too good for me,
a woman from the provinces but tall
and literate, of noble ancestry,
who makes herself available, a neck
ready to be touched, but no word
is said until I go to her and speak
as best I can a minor chord
that she is more the keeper of
than I, who've mastered nothing but a way
of holding her she likes, above
the waist, so I can go her length and play
what she's asking for, or try at least
to pull from her a sound that's sad and deep.

V

"Things could be better, Lloyd"

I have to change my life,
but how? What Rilke said
was beautiful and brief,
although he never said
exactly what to do.
Should I start drinking less
or maybe more? Should I
be kinder to my friends
or go into the woods?
Or should I start to read
*The Seven Habits of Highly
Effective People*
by that bald mountain man
who had a personal
relationship with Christ
and a mission statement
for his cringing family?
And then there is that book,
Dale Carnegie I think,
on how to stop worrying
and live the life that's mine.
But then I think the only
honest thing to do
is quote Jack Nicholson
in *The Shining*, out of his mind
but standing at the bar
and getting drinks for free
from Lloyd, who smiles a bit
but doesn't like to talk.

"Things could be better, Lloyd,
   a whole lot better."
   And after that he goes
   and swings the axe and kills
   poor Scatman Crothers,
   by which point everything
   has taken a turn for the worse,
   but that's the way of the world,
   no angels anywhere
   and a far cry, it's true,
   from the thing that Rilke said.

Fermi's Paradox

The contradiction between the probability of extraterrestrial life and our lack of contact with it led Enrico Fermi to ask the question, "Where is everybody?"

We sat together in the dark
and talked about those other worlds
Enrico Fermi thought might be
awash with aliens

because his numbers pointed up
the likelihood of teeming life
among the stars. But where, alas,
did everybody go?

You'd think, perhaps, the prodigies
would come to us or play upon
our signals and reciprocate
—though not if they were bugs.

It could be that they flamed out
the same way we might disappear,
in Malthusian catastrophes
we bring upon ourselves,

or maybe, by design, they've gone
to hide beyond Andromeda
because they realized long ago
how frequently we lie.

We're not worth knowing in the end,
a filthy, biomechanical,
weapons-bearing form of life
that builds amusement parks.

Of all the heavens haven't said,
the best by far I think is this,
that we, together in the dark,
aspire not to care.

Room

I used to live a simple life,
but it isn't possible anymore.
A monk's routine, a wooden chair,
some bread, the room, and a canteen
—it doesn't last for very long.
One falls in love, and children come
like giant offshore oil platforms,
and no more vespers then. Nothing
ever seems to be enough.
The work that I've committed to,
the costs I am obliged to pay,
are more expensive all around
than anything accounted for,
and the days, piling up, throw down
rocks and rusted metal pipes
that put paid to the charitable
and right-minded things I'd planned
to do or be. I've come to think
that maybe this is it then,
the room where I can live at last
with no lease of any kind,
and I will never have to leave.

The White-Breasted Nuthatch

Like a clerk in a local discount store
diligently counting every cent,
the bird asks for nothing more
than its small due, picking what scant
food it can from between the strips
of hardened bark it clings upside-
down to. Pine weevils and ants
make up the meal, and just outside
its hole it smears blister beetles
to irk the squirrel that likes to come
and try to kill it. On principle
it flicks feces from the nest at dawn.
In the bankrupting cold of wintertime
it tells me what, in fact, is mine.

Wild Turkeys

They hump like grunts in a long line
down out of the woods, all black
against the snow, and go behind
the house to a rally point out back
to eat from piles of corn feed
we put out there to ease their lot,
hoping that tonight at least
they won't starve. Some get shot
as a matter of course, others freeze
before the winter's out, some
are taken quickly by diseases
only the birds know, and some
troop on with their heads down,
not wanting to be found.

Night Heron

How badly I would like to say
some dulcet thing
about that most unknown
of birds, the hunched one hoarding
the only word it knows,
a *squark* or *squak* it gives up
when it goes away.

You'll come across it
in the dusk, intent
among the water weeds or stooped
in branches hard along a bank,
watchful but at peace,
getting you in its gimlet eye.

A right conveyance
(all that I aspire to)
calls for something common, crabbed,
and off by just enough
to meet the red-eyed soul
halfway along the ditch of what it is.

Taken by its task,
absorbed in telling beads
or praying quietly that fish
may always come,
the poor contrarian holds out a hope
that it's enough
to go on doing what we can.

Dog

Is that the thing you found today,
the little gewgaw that you love?
It's a piece of Day-Glo rubber ball
you ardently dug out of the snow.
You are, my friend, a quadruped
that eats dirt and runs around.
I put my face among your paws,
where all good smells originate,
and stroke the velvet of your ear.
Inside, it smells like cumin seeds.
Are you the Other? Is that the game?
Well, I have two legs, you have four,
your breath is lovely, mine is foul,
and I speak French, while you do not,
and you eat sticks, though I do not,
and so if I were doctrinaire
(the word "dogmatic" I'll resist),
I'd say that we're as far apart
as Cain and Abel ever were
and that we didn't have much hope
of ever being cheek by jowl.
And yet we're *always* cheek to jowl!
You soak up love the way a weed
takes all it wants of water and light.
You keep your tchotchke close to you
and gather yourself to go to sleep
on the couch that's practically yours now.
You live an unexamined life,
but that's OK, you are a dog,

and who will cast the first stone?
Your brown, pulchritudinous eyes
drink me in, and I am yours
and hope that you can smell this love
I carry around, no questions asked,
for you, my dear digger, sleeping
like a dog beside me now.

Woods

I took the dog and went to walk
in the auditorium of the woods,
but not to get away from things.
It was our habit, that was all,
a thing we did on summer days,
and much there was to listen to.
A slight wind came and went
in three birches by the pond.
A crow uphill was going on
about the black life it led,
and a brown creeper went creeping up
a brown trunk methodically
with no record of ever having
been understood by anyone.
A woodpecker was working out
a deep hole from the sound of it
in a stand of dead trees up there.
And then a jay, much put upon,
complained about some treachery
it may or may not have endured,
though most are liars anyway.
The farther in, the quieter,
till only the snapping of a stick
broke the silence we were in.
The dog stood still and looked at me,
the woods by then already dark.
Much later, on the porch at night,
I heard the owl, an eldritch thing.
The dog, still with me, heard it too,

a call that came from where we'd been
and where we would not be again.